SandCastle™
Giant Animals

PANDA

ANDERS HANSON

Consulting Editor, Diane Craig, M.A./Reading Specialist

A Division of ABDO

ABDO
Publishing Company

visit us at www.abdopublishing.com

Published by ABDO Publishing Company, a division of ABDO, P.O. Box 398166, Minneapolis, Minnesota 55439. Copyright © 2014 by Abdo Consulting Group, Inc. International copyrights reserved in all countries. No part of this book may be reproduced in any form without written permission from the publisher. SandCastle™ is a trademark and logo of ABDO Publishing Company.

Printed in the United States of America, North Mankato, Minnesota
102013
012014

 PRINTED ON RECYCLED PAPER

Editor: Liz Salzmann
Content Developer: Nancy Tuminelly
Cover and Interior Design and Production: Anders Hanson, Mighty Media, Inc.
Photo Credits: Shutterstock, Thinkstock

Library of Congress Cataloging-in-Publication Data
Hanson, Anders, 1980- author.
  Panda / Anders Hanson ; consulting editor, Diane Craig, M.A., reading specialist.
      pages cm. -- (Giant animals)
  Audience: 4 to 9.
  ISBN 978-1-62403-060-4
  1. Giant panda--Juvenile literature. I. Craig, Diane, editor. II. Title.
  QL737.C27H3923 2014
  599.789--dc23
                              2013023929

SandCastle™ Level: Transitional

SandCastle™ books are created by a team of professional educators, reading specialists, and content developers around five essential components—phonemic awareness, phonics, vocabulary, text comprehension, and fluency—to assist young readers as they develop reading skills and strategies and increase their general knowledge. All books are written, reviewed, and leveled for guided reading, early reading intervention, and Accelerated Reader® programs for use in shared, guided, and independent reading and writing activities to support a balanced approach to literacy instruction. The SandCastle™ series has four levels that correspond to early literacy development. The levels are provided to help teachers and parents select appropriate books for young readers.

Emerging Readers
(no flags)

Beginning Readers
(1 flag)

Transitional Readers
(2 flags)

Fluent Readers
(3 flags)

contents

HELLO, PANDA!

GIANT PANDA,
6 FEET (1.8 M)

Pandas are bears with black and white coats. They have round faces and big bodies.

PANDA CUB

HUMAN,
6 FEET
(1.8 M)

WHAT ARE YOU UP TO?

Pandas eat and sleep a lot. They seem **lazy**. But they are just saving **energy**. Having a big body is a lot of work!

COOL PATCHES!

Pandas are mostly white. They have **patches** of black fur around their eyes, ears, and legs.

ARE YOU CUDDLY?

Pandas look cute and **cuddly**. But remember that they are bears! They have sharp teeth and claws.

WHERE ARE YOU GOING?

Pandas are good climbers.
Sometimes they take naps in trees.

WHERE DO YOU LIVE?

Pandas live in China. They live where there are bamboo trees.

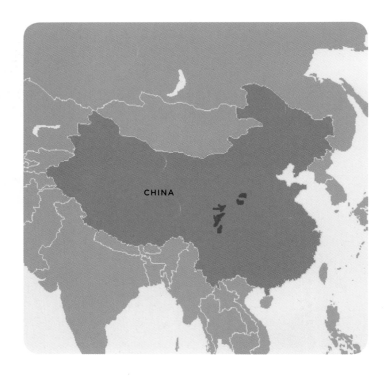

CHINA

WHAT DO YOU EAT?

Pandas eat mostly bamboo stems and leaves. Pandas eat about 25 pounds (11 kg) of bamboo each day!

DO YOU HAVE A FAMILY?

Panda cubs stay with their mothers for about two years. The cubs often play with each other. Pandas live alone when they grow up.

ARE YOU IN DANGER?

Pandas are **endangered**. The bamboo forests are getting smaller. They have less space to live and food to eat.

QUICK QUIZ

Check your answers below!

1. **Pandas are bears.** TRUE OR FALSE?

2. **Pandas don't sleep or eat a lot.** TRUE OR FALSE?

3. **Pandas live in China.** TRUE OR FALSE?

4. **Pandas mostly eat flowers.** TRUE OR FALSE?

1) True 2) False 3) True 4) False

GLOSSARY

cuddly – good to hold close because of being soft and warm.

endangered – close to extinction.

energy – the ability to move, work, or play hard without getting tired.

lazy – not willing to work or be active.

patch – a small area that is different from its surroundings.

Do not ride too close to parked cars. They might pull out suddenly. Car doors can open without warning. Follow these rules for a fun, safe ride.

Try It! Go back and look at the hand signals on pages 22 and 23. Now you try them!

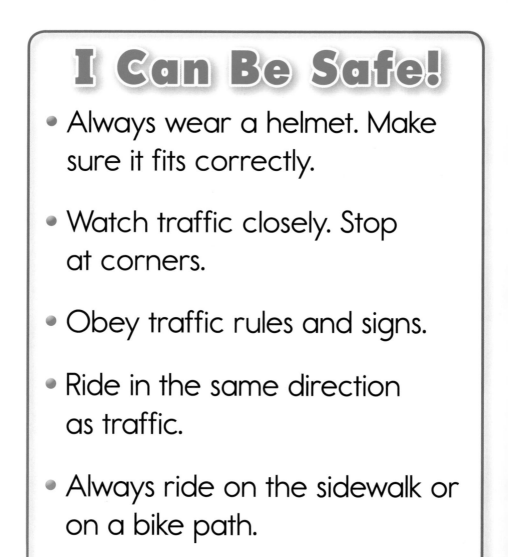

I Can Be Safe!

- Always wear a helmet. Make sure it fits correctly.

- Watch traffic closely. Stop at corners.

- Obey traffic rules and signs.

- Ride in the same direction as traffic.

- Always ride on the sidewalk or on a bike path.

Words You Know

bicycle

bike path

headphones

helmet

Index

Facts for Now

Visit this Scholastic Web site for more information on bicycle safety:
www.factsfornow.scholastic.com
Enter the keyword **Bicycle**

About the Author

Lisa M. Herrington writes print and digital materials for kids, teachers, and parents. She lives in Connecticut with her husband and daughter. She hopes all kids stay safe!